Don't Name Your Baby
What's Wrong with Every Name in the Book

David Narter

Cumberland House
Nashville, Tennessee

DON'T NAME YOUR BABY
PUBLISHED BY CUMBERLAND HOUSE PUBLISHING, INC.
431 Harding Industrial Drive
Nashville, Tennessee 37211-3160

Copyright © 2001 by David Narter

All rights reserved. Written permission must be secured from the publisher
to use or reproduce any part of this book, except brief quotations in critical
reviews or articles.

Cover design: Unlikely Suburban Design
Text design: Lisa Taylor

Library of Congress Cataloging-in-Publication Data

Narter, David, 1965–
    Don't name your baby : what's wrong with every name in the book /
David Narter.
    p. cm.
    ISBN 13 978-1-58182-208-3 (pbk. : alk. paper)
    ISBN 10 1-58182-208-1 (pbk. : alk. paper)
    1. Names, Personal—Dictionaries. I. Title.
CS2377.N36 2001
    929.4'4'03—dc21   2001028597

Printed in the United States of America
3 4 5 6 7 8 — 11 10 09 08 07 06

For my children, # and π

Contents

Introduction

Before our first child was born, my ex-wife and I engaged in every prenatal ritual from the mundane to the absurd. We sonogrammed, stroller shopped, read up on *Spock* and created list after list of possible baby names. One thing we found from our many revisions is that a strong argument can be made against any name. Michael is overused, Lucas rhymes with mucous, and Max is a dog. Nancy is boring, Candy's a porn star, Sylvia's old, and (if you've seen *Willy Wonka*) Violet is violet! We found that list reduction was as much a part of the naming game as the seeking out of new, original, and often stupid names.

And for good reason. The name you give your baby will be so much of a part of that child that, years from now, he'll find much of his personality has been defined by the name. And even if you choose not to take naming so seriously, others will—and your kid will pay the price (most likely with a good ass-kicking) for your shortsightedness. So choose wisely.

A sort of divine providence guarantees a relationship—corollary, causal or inverse—between a name and a child. In second grade, I ate lunch with a kid named Mike Cutlip, who seemed every day to cut his lip on everything from plastic knives to napkins. I recall three separate occasions on which poor Mike ran from the cafeteria, blood gushing from beneath a wad of brown paper towels held to

Introduction

his face after he had somehow sliced his bottom lip on a milk carton. Three times! Surely his unfortunate surname, at least as much as his thin skin, contributed to his hard luck.

But first names are our concern here, and, for me, the relationship between misfortune and moniker has always appeared just as strong. The stinkiest kid in my junior high school was named Ivory, a boy further tormented by the fact that his skin was jet black. The irony on both counts didn't escape anyone in the eighth grade, and Ivory was reminded of it daily. On the other hand, the best body in the boy's locker room belonged to Adonis Reed. Determined not to be the butt of the same sort of jokes Ivory endured, Adonis spent five days a week in the conditioning gym (and eventually jail) developing his physique. Adonis's insecurity ultimately led him to steroids, and today he is a hairless, sterile linebacker with a gruff disposition. Kids named Randy tend to be randy. Harrys are almost never bald, and those who are find themselves plagued by the inescapable irony.

Naming a child may very well invoke some mystical force, reshaping bodies and minds, and changing predestined paths. Or perhaps, like Adonis, children are all too aware of the implications of their names and do their best to live up to or, more commonly, rebel against them. All of us know at least one person ashamed of her first name and going by another. We all know a girl named Birgut or Gretchen who grew up dreading that first day of class when the teacher would call her name and everyone would turn to see where the ugly girl was. Or maybe a Myron or Dexter who had

Don't Name Your Baby

no choice but to study computer programming between playground beatings. Call it predestination or self-fulfilling prophecy; a lousy name is almost always the doorway to a lousy childhood.

None of this is news to anyone over six. So most parents put plenty of time into choosing a name. And that is the fool's errand that has brought you to this book. As if somewhere between the mundane and ridiculous lies a name that not only represents your unique spirit, but will also assure your child a second grade of comradery and confidence. Forget it. People are going to harass your kid no matter what you call him. Every name and every naming strategy is doomed.

The Maverick
Yeah, you want your kid to have an original, inimitable name. Something like Edison or Steinam. A name that will tell the world and all the people in the subdivision what a hip, enlightened thinker you are. A name that will set your kid apart from the rest of the crowd. But remember that kids who stand alone at recess are usually the ones most often teased and beat up.

The Social Climber
The most desperate practice, and one that has been around since Julius Caesar (and a lot of baby Juliuses), is naming your child one or two social classes above yourself. The nineties saw names like Courtney, Ashley, and Brittany, once considered too pretentious to be called from the porch of a ranch house, being shouted out the

Introduction

windows of minivans and across the rolling soccer fields of suburbia. Soon these names will be synonymous with the likes of Star Wars mythology and the Macarena—in hindsight so absurd and pedestrian that we have to ask ourselves, "How could we have thought that was cool?"

Down on the Farm

In the movement toward a renewed appreciation for simplicity and nature, plenty of names that had long since been sent out to stud have reappeared in recent years. Zachs, Zanes, and Codys feud Shanes and Travises for control of the schoolyard posse. But when Shane hangs up his saddle and hat and is bagging groceries in a food-stained apron, his nametag will look as ridiculous as a bald guy named Curley.

Playing It Safe

Of course this isn't a solution either. Plenty of Karens and Mikes complain of having no sense of personal identity other than that they are the Karen with blonde hair or the Mike who is tall. These are the sort of people who memorize their social security and driver's license numbers as if grateful that somebody—even if it's the DMV—chose to see them as individuals.

The Latest Thing

So you choose the quirky, yet fashionable names of the day. Jessica and Jason become Amber and Sam. But your plans are thwarted

Don't Name Your Baby

when you register little Max for kindergarten and hear the teacher mutter under her breath, "Oh, *please* not another Max."

It ought to be clear to you now, young parent-to-be, that the only solution is to not name your child at all.

As a rule, most of the psychological damage will occur during the tender years of elementary school. Thus, many of the entries in this book contain the likely nickname your child will pick up in the cafeteria or the playground. It might give you pause to think that the child you'll call Ralph will by known to his schoolmates as Puke.

Along the same lines are the Timeless Schoolyard Chants, tunes that have survived the test of time, bruising egos and breaking spirits for generations. Who could forget the ageless strains of "Barry the Fairy" or "Raggy Maggy?" Certainly not Barry or Maggy.

Often the strongest argument against the use of a name is its history and origin. When you actually put some thought into names like Taylor and Parker (one who sews and one who parks), they tend to lose a bit of their pretense.

Also provided, you'll find references to popular culture that are simply unavoidably attached to some names. Your Tanya may as well be a weeping, knee-bashing Tonya Harding, since that's what others will see when they meet her. Tabatha is Samantha Stevens's daughter, Jan is Jan Brady, and Marcia . . . Marcia, Marcia, Marcia! These associations, annoying as they may be, are ubiquitous and can't help but ring in the ears like tornado sirens. If they didn't come to mind before, they will now.

Introduction

You'll find that you will come to use this book not only for baby planning, but to occasionally put that kid who walks through your lawn every morning in his place. You may even want to retake the second grade just to try out a few taunts in the proper arena.

In the end I think you'll agree, as my ex-wife and I eventually did, that naming your baby is a pretty cruel way to introduce a kid to the world.

Girls' Names

Abigail/Abby

A name that died with the last Pilgrim and somehow has risen like a foul New England ghost. Prithee, good fellow, selectith elsewhere. *Likely nicknames:* Crabby, Flabby, Scabby.

Adrian

Yo, Adrian! Hope you like lame Stallone impressions. You're going to hear a lot of them.

Adriana

A name used exclusively for little girls who start out as Adrians but become too snotty.

Agatha

Likely nickname: Ragatha.

Agnes

Likely nickname: Ragness.

Girls' Names

Aimee

Oh, how original! This doesn't seem at all like Amy! It's like a totally new name!

Alex/Alexandra/Alexis

Cold as a chandelier and understated as a tiara on a drag queen. Names that reek diamonds and fur. Most girls with these names do not actually adopt them until they are post-menopausal and mean.

Ali

Floats like a butterfly, stings like a bee.

Alice

Alices tend to marry Ralphs. So until Ralph picks up, you might want to avoid this one.

Alicia

The female version of a female name. Now what is the sense of that? Girls named Alicia know they are just dressed-up Alices and consequently grow up angry and resentful.

Don't Name Your Baby

Allie
The space between two buildings on which one drives a car, tosses out garbage, or vomits after drinking too much. Famous Allies include Tin Pan Alley, Skid Row, and bowling alley.

Allison
What does this name mean? Son of Alice? Shouldn't this be a boy's name?

Alyssa
Ali, Alice, Allison, Alyssa, enough already! Turn the page!

Amanda
A man what? Your baby's a man? What?

Amber
Royal herald of The Minivan Royalty. Amber has as her responsibility to guard the soccer balls and protect Queen Brittany of the Desperately Pretentious Suburban Elite (see page 50).

Amelia
Roughly translates from Latin as "working on it" or "striv-

Virgin Mary Sightings

Madonna may have started something here! Naming her daughter Lourdes after the commune in the South of France where Mary occasionally stops for a visit could be the first step in the next Madonna craze. Remember that whole business of wearing undergarments on the outside of clothes? Is this any less probable? Surely the economies of these towns will appreciate the free publicity. And the educational benefits are obvious . . . aren't they? Naming your child after one of these towns in which Mary has been sighted will be good for business, promote cultural awareness, and most important, add some more unique names to our ever needy American lexicon.

Akita
Cankton
Cuapa
Eisenberg
Gortnodreha
Janonis
Lubbock

Naju
Turzovka
Zarvanystya
Zeitun

Don't Name Your Baby

ing to get better." Amelias suffer from inferiority complexes and never quite live up to their parents' expectations.

Amy
Amy has such a cutesy, juvenile feel that most girls named Amy never get promoted past third grade. *Likely nickname:* Lamey.

Anabel
Likely nicknames: Anabel the cannibal, Anabel the mandible, Handable.

Andrea
Oh my God! Means "manly" in Greek. *Likely nickname:* Mandrea.

Angel
Meow. *See* Names Your Baby Will Never Live Up To.

Angela
City of Angels, Angels in the Outfield, Touched by an Angel: haven't we had enough of this angel crap already?

Girls' Names

Angelica

Means "like an angel," implying that your daughter is not quite an angel. Has the same effect as names like Quasibeauty or Prettyish.

Anita

Means "little Anne." Boy, this name's going to be uncomfortable come puberty if she's a chub! Timeless schoolyard chant:
Anita, Anita, the sexy senorita.

Anna

Timeless schoolyard chant:
Anna, Anna,_____ my banana.
(insert verb here)

Anne

Since this will undoubtedly be your choice for her middle name (it's everyone else's), maybe you should avoid it for a first name for fear you'll accidentally name your girl Anne Anne.

April

People who name children after the month of their birth aren't saying a lot for their baby's intelligence or long-term

Don't Name Your Baby

memory. Or if she isn't born in April, what are you trying to do? Confuse her?

Ariel
Likely nickname: Scariel.

Ashley
Princess of the Minivan Royalty. Should Brittany be unable to perform her duties as Queen of the Desperately Pretentious Suburban Elite, Ashley will rule in her stead (see page 50).

No, it's Aubrey. A-U-B-R-E-Y. B! B! B!

Asia
Not quite a name so much as a crowded continent on which no one is named Asia.

Aubrey
The name clearly originated on a misspelled birth certificate. Your Aubrey will have to spend far too much of her life correcting people, and she'll eventually just change her name to Audrey anyway.

Girls' Names

Audrey
Audreys usually feel so bad about the whole Aubrey problem that they call themselves Claire.

Bailey
Along with Haley, shares a position as herald in the court of the Daycare Sovereignty. Baileys and Haleys will bow and tip their juice boxes when Courtney and Lyndsey pass (see page 50).

Barbara
Means "strange." A popular name for famous women in the sixties. It's hard to think of this name without thinking of bouffant hairdos.

Becky
Nobody names their kid Becky. It's just an unfortunate thing that happens to girls named Rebecca.

Beth
People will think she has a lisp.

Bethany
Means "house of poverty."

Don't Name Your Baby

Betty

Bettys wear aprons and spend far too much time worrying about spots on their silverware. Bettys live in ranch-style houses and make pot roast on Thursday. I wish my mom were a Betty.

Bianca

Means "white." What are 'ya? Some kind of racist or something?

Blaine

Plain Blaine.

Blair

Means "flat." That's going to hurt come puberty.

Bonnie

Means "pretty;" ironic, since the name is about as attractive on a girl as a pastel radioactive suit.

Brandi/Brandy

"You're a fine girl. What a good wife you would be." You're going to name your daughter after a top-forty song about an easy barmaid?

Breanna/Breanne/Breanon/Brynne

As if Brian were so attractive a name it should have been feminized. Like reshaping dried Play-Doh.

Brenda

A husky, horse-mouth of a name.

Bridget

Ooh la la. A name that reeks of cheap perfume and unwashed underclothes. *Likely nickname:* The frigid midget.

Brittany

Queen of the Minivan Royalty, Ruler of The Desperately Pretentious Suburban Elite and archenemy of Courtney, Queen of the Daycare Sovereignty. Most Brittanys live in extra-fancy trailer parks (see page 50).

Brooke

Likely nickname: Babbling Brooke.

Caitlin/Caitlinn/Caitlyn/Kaitlin/Kaitlyn/Katelyn, etc.

That's great! Only five other girls on the block are named Caitlin! She'll fit right in! How the heck are you supposed to spell this name anyway?

Names for Ugly Girls

Sometimes an ugly baby and a name just go together. We advise putting at least one of these names on your list just in case junior arrives as a passenger on the homely bus. Conversely, prenaming a baby one of these gems has been known to assist in the uglification process. In the end, no one will know whether you were proactive or reactive—only that you named your baby well.

Claudette	Lorraine	Sonia
Eunice	Mariam	Tania
Frances	Myra	Ursula
Frida	Pam	Uma
Gertrude	Pat	Uta
Gretchen	Paula	Violet
Hester	Prudence	Winfred
Hilda	Quinn	Yolanda
Hortense	Ramona	Yvonne
Ingrid	Rhonday	Zelda
Jody	Roseanne	

Girls' Names

Callie/Cally

Try saying this name without sounding like you have a speech impediment. Now what are you going to do when she really does? Don't tempt the gods of irony.

Cameron

Likely nickname: Cammy pajammy. Actually, that sounds pretty cute. Okay, try this one: Spameron. Now that's humiliating!

Camille

Timeless schoolyard chant:
> *Camille, Camille,*
> *Lemme cop a feel!*

Candace

I want Candy! I want Candy! At thirty, when she wants to be taken seriously in the business world, Candace will inevitably be taken down a notch when a co-worker refers to her as Candy.

Cara/Kara

Sounds like half a name.

Don't Name Your Baby

Carla/Karla

A thick, heavy, lumbering name that pours out of the mouth like gooey maple syrup. It'll cover your baby like wet clay.

Carly

Means "manly" in Old German.

Carmen

Does the image of a full-figured woman with a hatful of fruit come to mind? It ought to.

Carol

An all-purpose girl's name. Handy for those times you don't know what to call a girl, Carol will do. As dependable and practical as a ten-pound girdle.

Caroline

Essentially, Caroline is Carol with new curtains and fresh paint. But underneath, it's still Carol.

Girls' Names

Carrie

What first comes to mind is an adolescent witch with popularity problems. What next comes to mind is a bucket of pig blood. *Likely nickname:* Hairy Carrie.

Casey

Chuga, chuga. Chuga, chuga. Chuga, chuga. Woo! Woo!

Cassandra

Means "unheeded fortune teller." Beautiful, no?

> I like ponies. They're pretty.

Cassidy

Sean or David?

Catherine

Every eighth-grade boy has heard the rumors about Catherine the Great and her horse. Girls named Catherine are the first people they tell.

Chastity

Wishful thinking.

Don't Name Your Baby

Chelsea
The Amy [Carter] of the 90s. This name bears the irreparable scars that only an adolescence as the president's daughter can cause.

Cheryl
For the powerless girl. Smooth and soft, Cheryl is as confrontational as a tub of whipped cream or a feather pillow. Cheryls don't get too far in school or at work, but no one ever hated a Cheryl. Of course, most people aren't aware they've ever met a Cheryl.

Cheyenne/Cherokee
How arrogantly chic to name your daughter after a nation of people your country conquered.

Chloe
Zowie!

Christian
A religion, not a name. Ever meet a girl named Jewish or a boy named Buddhist?

Girls' Names

Christine/Christina

She'll eventually want to be called Chris. And face it, Chris is a boy's name! Boy's name!

Celeste

Likely nickname: Celeste the chest.

Cindy/Cynthia

Most often associated with the youngest of the Brady girls, a lispy, pigtailed, grating sort of name that on a woman of fifty wears like Betty Davis's make-up job in *What Ever Happened to Baby Jane?*

Claire/Clare

Timeless schoolyard chant:
> *Scary Claire,*
> *sounds like a bear,*
> *looks like Rover,*
> *and smells like underwear.*

Claudia

Perhaps the saddest example of a man's name with a cheap sex-change operation since Fredrica. Claudia feels as heavy and awkward as a wrestler in a tutu.

Don't Name Your Baby

Cleopatra
Oh, get over yourself! What are you, in denial? Get it? De' Nile? Ah hah hah hah hah!!!

Coco
A good name for a dog.

Colleen
Famous Colleens include Lassie and Son of Lassie.

Courtney
Queen of the Daycare Sovereignty and archenemy of Brittany, Queen of the Minivan Royalty. Courtney and Brittany have been in a decade-long battle for rule over The Desperately Pretentious Suburban Elite (see page 50).

Crystal
You're going to name your baby after a shiny rock? Hey, everybody has money troubles, but you can't be that desperate. Show a little dignity.

Cynthia
At thirty, when she wants to be taken seriously in the business world, Cynthia will

Names for Octogenarian Babies

Does your little princess smell like lilac perfume? Does your little slugger have more hair in his nose and ears than on his head? Probably not. Apparently motives for choosing these dinosaurs have more to do with money than baby himself. For instance, AARP will reportedly send out a free discount card to parents who name their babies from this list. And according to *Senior Magazine*, 5000 wills were rewritten last year by delighted grandparents happy to see their names back in circulation.

GIRLS
Beatrice
Betty
Getrude
Gladys
Harriet
Hazel
Josephine
Lois
Louise
Lucille
Mabel
Madge

Nora
Ruth
Sally
Sylvia
Velma
Vivian
Wilhelmina

BOYS
Abraham
Albert
Amos
Charlie

Ernie
Eugene
George
Harold
Lloyd
Maurice
Norman
Ralph
Ruben
Sam
Sheldon
Stuart
Walter

inevitably be taken down a notch when a co-worker refers to her as Cindy.

Daisy
A flower, a duck, not a girl.

Dakota
How arrogantly chic to name your daughter after a nation of people your country conquered.

Danielle
Daniel in drag, wearing a beret.

Dawn
Frankie Valli said it best when he sang, "Dawn, go away. Please, go away!"

Deanna
Originated by parents with a limited sense of imagination who wanted to name their kids something other than Diana.

Deborah
Likely nickname (if well-endowed): Da Bra.

Girls' Names

Deirdre
Made famous by Deirdre of Sorrows of Irish mythology who managed to get everybody in the country killed because of her bad attitude.

Deja
Most kids named Deja are greeted with "Oh, no! Not that kid again!"

Denise
Derived from the Greek god of wine and debauchery, Dionysus, but also translates as "the lame god." Could be a combination of the two implying a sort of divine impotence.

Destiny
Oh, please! It's just a baby!

Diana
The virgin goddess of hunting and childbirth, Diana was mainly worshiped by peasants who knew the value of a good fertility god. Diana tended to be bad-tempered, like when she unleashed a wild boar upon a village because she was feeling unloved. Who needs that kind of aggravation?

Don't Name Your Baby

Diane
"Diane's sitting on Jackie's lap. She's got his hands between her knees." Yeah, that's the image you want of your little princess.

Dinah
Timeless schoolyard chant:
> Dinah won't you blow, Dinah won't you blow, Dinah won't you blow my _____?
>> (fill in the blank)

Donna
Means "lady." Upon traveling to Europe, your Donna will evoke nothing but confusion and annoyance when introducing herself.

Drew
The past tense of "draw."

Dylan
Originally a verb referring to a pickling process. So who are you naming your baby after, the alcoholic poet or the alcoholic singer?

Girls' Names

Ebony

What are you—racist or something?

Edith

Eat it!

Eileen

Timeless schoolyard joke: You know the only thing more disgusting than Olivia Newton John in *Grease*? "Come on Eileen." A hah hah hah hah!!!

Elaine

Likely nickname: Smelaine.

Eleanor

Likely nickname: Smellanor.

Elizabeth

A once graceful and noble name that has been chopped and reprocessed into so many American pieces that it now resembles its old self as much as American cheese resembles a dairy product. Choosing a name with so many derivatives is like letting your baby choose her own name. Maybe she'll pick Betty!

Don't Name Your Baby

Ella
Likely nickname: Smella.

Ellen
Rotund and wobbly as a watermelon. *Likely nickname:* Smellin' Ellen.

Emily
A mushy, meek, and furry name that even kittens find nauseating. She's not going to be a baby forever.

Emma
The federal government consigned one Emma to each woman of childbearing age in 1995. Any further Emmas require a doctor's note and the consent of your state representative.

Erica
Eric with a cheap sex change.

Erin
Erin, go brahless!

Girls' Names

Esther

Likely nickname: Esther the molester.

Eve/Eva

It is difficult for men to meet women named Eve without picturing them naked.

Evelyn

Likely nickname: Elephant.

Faith

Why don't you just tattoo a big cross on her face?

Fawn

One in a string of names that in the nineties was soiled like a blue party dress. Move on.

Felicia

Cop a cheap Felicia!

Fiona

Pee on ya!

Don't Name Your Baby

Frances
A mule.

G
A word about G names: they're all ugly.

Gabrielle/Gabriella
No teacher ever liked a girl named Gabby.

Geena/Gina
Weena!

Georgia
Hate crimes capital of the South!

Gigi
A flowery, high-heeled name. Perfect for a girl destined to walk the streets.

Ginger
Mmm. Now that's sexy. Yeah. Your baby's going to have a sexy name. . . . What kind of freak are you?!

Girls' Names

Giselle

Isn't that some kind of African animal?

Gloria

I think they got your number! Glorias tend to get conceited around Christmastime.

Grace

In grade school cafeterias, Graces are the students most often tripped. This action is then followed by the classic, "Been to charm school, Grace?"

Gretchen

Timeless schoolyard chant:
Gretch, Gretch, makes me retch.

Haley

Along with Bailey, shares a position as herald in the court of the Daycare Sovereignty. Haleys and Baileys will bow and tip their juice boxes when Courtney and Lyndsey pass.

Hannah

Timeless schoolyard chant:
Hannah, Hannah, _____ my banana.
(insert verb here)

Don't Name Your Baby

Harley
You're going to name your daughter after a motorcycle ridden primarily by filthy, overweight losers?

Heather
Ugly stepsister of Ashley, Princess of the Minivan Royalty. Banned from the daycare tower for thinking she's "all that," Heather is now a highly esteemed member of The Trailer Park Underground (see page 50).

Heidi
Pigtailed, jackbooted tomboy of children's books, without whom this horribly ugly name would have disappeared years ago.

Helen
An all-purpose, heavy-duty, one-gallon–size girl name, handy for those times you don't know what to call a girl. As dutifully practical as a can of oven cleaner.

Hillary
Either way, people have their minds pretty well made up about this one. Why put your daughter in the middle of all that?

Girls' Names

Holly

Classic Christmas taunt: *Deck the halls with bowzer Holly!*

Hope

Makes *you* seem desperate.

Ilene

You certainly do.

India

Not so much a name as it is a country where no one is named India.

Iris

How 'bout Retina?

Isabel

Is a bell? I dunno. Is a? *Likely nickname:* Isabel the witch from hell.

Jackie

Mothers in the sixties wore this name out. It is now as fashionable as a powder blue pillbox hat.

Don't Name Your Baby

Jamie
   A little boy name. Jamies are perky and short but can't grow breasts.

Jane
   Plain Jane.

Janelle
   The female form of Jane, a female name. For extra-female females.

Janet
   Damn it, Janet! If it wasn't a cool name in 1978, what makes you think it is now? Is Brad?

Jasmine
   Very popular among children who smell.

Jenna
   Half a name. Not quite Jennifer.

Jennifer
   During the eighties, all girls not named Jennifer were assigned the name Jessica. Time to give this one a rest.

Girls' Names

Jessica

During the nineties, all girls not named Jessica were assigned the name Jennifer. Better give this one a rest, too. *Likely nickname:* Chestica.

Jessy/Jesse/Jessey

Likely nickname: Chesty!

Jill

Likely nicknames: Jilly willy, Jilly beans, Jill the pill.

Joanna

They'll call her Joe. Just like you call your trashman Joe and the fella at the service station Joe.

Jodi

A name for round-faced, pug-nosed tomboys. Most Jodis can kick your ass.

Jordan

You're naming your little girl after a 220-pound male athlete? Have you considered Butkis? How about Larry or Wilt? Kobie?

Don't Name Your Baby

Josie
You say *Josie*, the world thinks hot pants and pussycats!

Joy
Most Joys tend to be foul-
tempered little brats.

Judith/Judy
A name made famous by
an enabling puppet and
victim of spousal abuse.

Julia
Is it at all pretentious or
wasteful that a five-letter word should tie
up three syllables?

Julie
Likely nicknames: Fooly, Ghouhly, Muley, Hoolie Hoopie.

Juliette
Most often associated with an overly dramatic adolescent
who wasn't smart enough to stick to her own kind.

Girls' Names

Justine
Likely nicknames: Crustine, Saltine, Ovaltine, Bactine.

Kaitlin
Oh, just see the entry for Caitlin. For crying out loud, it's all the same name.

Kali
Sounds like a kale-based juice drink. Yuck.

Kara
Oh, just see the entry for Cara. It's all the same name.

Karen
So overused in the 1950s that teachers in all-girl schools would often find themselves teaching an entire classroom of Karens. Consequently, most Karens older than forty are accustomed to introducing themselves as "Karen15" or "Karen23."

Kate
Naming your child a short derivative of a longer name is humiliating and can lead to permanent self-esteem issues.

Don't Name Your Baby

Katherine

Every eighth-grade boy has heard the rumors about Catherine the Great and her horse. Girls named Katherine are the first people they tell.

Katie

Naming your child a cutesy, short derivative of a longer name is like telling her to just shut up and smile about it.

Kaylee

This name originated when a father threw a bunch of letters in the air and went with whatever combination they landed in.

Kelly

As classy as sticking a permanent "Kiss Me, I'm Irish" bumper sticker on your baby's face. *Likely nickname:* Smelly.

Kelsey

A dark, amber beer with a thick head and heavy finish. Kelsey and chips are popular among toothless soccer fans.

Girls' Names

Kendall
Ken doll?

Kennedy
If democrats are going to keep naming their babies Kennedy, then Republicans are bound to start naming theirs Bush.

Keri
Likely nickname: Hairy Keri.

Kim
Kim sits upon girls with any bit of personality like a tiny head on a fat woman.

Kimberly
All the allure and grace of a girdle.

Kirsten/Kirsta/Krista
Most parents cleverly turn to these hybrid names when their first choice, Kristen, has already been taken. Their

Thank God they weren't Bush supporters.

Don't Name Your Baby

daughters aren't fooled by this slight of hand and suffer self-esteem issues that only heighten when they meet girls who are really named Kristen.

Kristen
Most Kristens feel so bad about the whole Kirsten/Kirsta thing they change their name to Patsy.

Kylie
A ridiculous attempt to squeeze one more name out of the letter K.

Lacey
A word most often paired with "undergarment." For most men, Lacey brings to mind Victoria's Secret catalogues and half-naked models . . . oh, and now your baby.

Lakeisha, Latasha, Latifa, Latoya, Laverne
Just Keisha, Tasha, Tifa, Toya, and Verne with a "La" in front—nothing more.

Lara
As if getting rid of the "u" makes this name somehow more exotic.

Laura

Old dependable. As ordinary and comfortable as a well-worn vinyl recliner.

Leah

Biblical history: Rachel's ugly sister that Jacob is tricked into marrying. Means "wild cow." Moo. Moo.

Leigh

What every teenage boy's looking to get.

Leslie/Lezlee

Sounds close enough to lesbian to cause her some stress in junior high.

Lily

Pretty flower, ugly name. A name suited to jolly, round collectors of porcelain dolls.

Linda

A real workhorse. Sturdy and dependable. A name that's hung in there through some long, hard times. Why, during the early seventies, it seemed to be just Linda, Carol,

Don't Name Your Baby

Karen, and Laura out there getting all that naming done. She's worked hard. Maybe it's time to give the old girl a rest.

Lindsey

Princess of the Daycare Sovereignty. Should Courtney be unable to perform her duties as Queen, Lindsey will rule in her stead (see page 50).

Lisa

The older boys will say, "I need a piece 'a Lisa!"

Logan

Dead by thirty.

Lori

For girls not attractive or clean enough for the formal Laura, this name will do.

Lourdes

Would you be considered too fanatical to name your child after a place in which locals claim Virgin Mary has appeared? Maybe people wouldn't think it was nearly so zealous if instead they just thought you were naming your baby after Madonna's. Yeah, that's not nutty.

The Unhappy Lineage and Rivalry
of
The Desperately Pretentious Suburban Elite

Minivan Royalty

Brittany
(Queen)

Ashley
(Princess)

Amber
(Royal Herald)

Skylar
(Court Magician)

Daycare Sovereignty

Courtney
(Queen)

Lindsey
(Princess)

Bailey/Haley
(Royal Herald)

Summer
(Court Magician)

The Trailer Park Underground (banished)

Heather
(older, yet identical step-sister of Amber,
for thinking she's "all that")

Tiffany
(for being "two-faced" and "bossy")

Don't Name Your Baby

Mackenzie
What is it that's inspiring you? The drug-addicted girl or the drug-addicted dog?

Madeline
Means "bad-tempered little thing."

Madison
Here's one that has no business being a girl's name. It's the last name of a perpetually angry president who suffered from short-man's syndrome, and before 1980, no poor girl had to deal with it. Somehow Madison caught on after it showed up in the film *Splash* as the mermaid's name. C'mon, that has to be the dumbest name origin in this book.

Madonna
Is it possible that a single person has worn out an entire name?

Maggy
Timeless schoolyard chant:
> *Raggy Maggy, her boobs are big and saggy.*

Girls' Names

Mallory
Means "bad luck."

Mandi/Mandy
You're going to name your daughter after a 70s pop song about Barry Manilow's dog? What kind of freak are you?

Look at me, Bouncing Baby Matilda!

Margaret
Go ahead. She'll just call herself Peggy.

Maria/Mariah/Marie/Marisa
All of these names are really just Mary. You're not fooling anyone. Giving your girl this name is like giving her a lifetime supply of faux-designer perfume.

Mary
Mary, of course, is a beautiful name, and the life of a young Mary can be very fine indeed. Just ask any of the girls born in the last fifty years, all of whom are named Mary. There is, however, one hitch worth noting: most

Don't Name Your Baby

baby books list the name Polly among the many Mary derivations. Now, as harrowing as that sounds, the prognosis is good. Ninety-five percent of all Marys will manage to avoid contracting Polly and live a relatively normal life. However, for those few Marys and their parents who are not so lucky, life can be very hard indeed.

Maureen
Likely nickname: Maureen the moron.

Megan/Meagan/Meghan/Mehgan
Girls named Megan want to be called Mehgan, and girls called Mehgan want to be called Megan. The rest of the world just wishes parents would quit naming their kids Mehgan . . . or Megan.

Melanie
They'll call her Mel. Be prepared for that. *Likely nickname:* Smelanie.

Melinda
Likely nickname: Smelinda.

Girls' Names

Melissa

Likely nickname: Smelissa.

Melody

Likely nickname: Smelody.

Mercedes

Desperate! If you don't have a Mercedes, you must really be pathetic.

Mia

When she introduces herself, everyone in daycare will think she's being selfish.

Michelle

Get ready for all your annoying in-laws and their lame Beatle imitations: "Michelle, my belle. Sonne a mon ta blah, yuck, chamba wu. Kie chamba wu."

Mindy

Fortunately, Mindy's first boyfriend will be a computer

What were they thinking? We can't even afford a Jetta.

Mercedes

Don't Name Your Baby

whiz. Unfortunately, the couple will be called Dork and Mindy.

Miranda

Most commonly associated with the right to remain silent. Your daughter is most likely to encounter her name at the end of *Starsky and Hutch* episodes. Then again, she may find her Miranda rights come in handy in the back of a squad car. *Interesting astronomical fact:* Miranda encircles Uranus!—the whole thing!

Molly

Good golly! She sure like to ball! Most Mollys have floppy ears, attract flies, and like to chase cars.

Monica

Likely nickname: Harmonica.

Morgan

Boy's name! Boy's name!

Nancy

Most commonly associated with the insult, "Nancy boy." The origin of this name is unclear, but we are sure that Nancy doesn't mean "strong" in any language.

Naomi

Too many vowels. Sounds whiney.

Natalie

Means "birthy." Natalies tend to stay bald and purple well into their teens and often wear little caps to cover their pointy skulls.

Natasha

Excellent choice, comrade. Upon her exit from the hospital, we will insert the microfilm into her diaper and have her shipped to the Kremlin.

Nicole

A name traditionally given to the lowest priced prostitute in a brothel.

Nina

Timeless schoolyard chant:

Nina, Nina. She'll _____ your weena.

(insert verb here)

Don't Name Your Baby

Noel

Good name if too many kids on your block are already named Halloween or Thanksgiving.

Olivia

I amsk what I amsk, Olivsk, and that's all that I amsk. Eh geh geh geh.

Opal

People who name their kids after precious gems seem desperate. They often accidentally write "Lotto" on the birth certificate.

Paige

Means "servant." Aim a little higher.

Pam

So flat and androgynous a name that most Pams find they are unable to grow breasts.

Pat

If Pam is an A cup, Pat is a sports bra.

Babies That Come with a Scent

The sad truth is that babies, if not washed regularly, can really stink up a house. Babies smell best on the top of their heads mostly because that's the only part of their bodies not expelling some vile, sour fluid every couple of hours. With the odor circus heading your way, the last thing you want to do is come home with a reeking birth certificate as well. While baby will eventually be able to hold down his milk, he'll never shake off a putrid name.

BOYS
Alfred - Mothballs
Brock - Grecian Formula
Chad/Chance/Chase - Lavoris and cocaine
Clinton - Teflon
Giovanni - Brut
Joe - Truck exhaust
Max - Dog bisquits
Ruben - Onion
Sheldon/Sidney/Stanley - Fried liver
Todd - Ivory Soap
Travis - Cow manure
Wayne - Wet tweed

GIRLS
Ashley - Strawberry perfume
Brittany - Apple lipstick
Cheyanne - Buffalo
Gretchen - Stuffed saugage
Helen - Furniture polish
Kali - Zucchini
Pam/Pat - Nothing
Raquel - Sex, raw sex
Shirley - Burgers and fries
Sydney - Denture cream
Tiffany - Cherry eyeliner
Tracy - Bubbles

Don't Name Your Baby

Paula
Comes in handy if you find you've incorrectly determined your child's gender as male. Most states will allow up to three months to add an "a" to Paul's birth certificate.

Penelope
Best known for fending off suitors while Ulysses was getting it on with every nymph, girl, and goat in Ancient Greece. Scholars believe the name translates as "one who got dissed" or "sucker."

Penny
Oh, that's good. Or maybe quarter or half-dollar?

Peyton
A place. Not a name.

Priscilla
Latin for "prissy little brat."

Prudence
Like all virtues, prudence is a drag.

Girls' Names

Rachel
Ancient Hebrew term referring to a female sheep. Baaaa.

Raquel
While most babies come home from the hospital with a complimentary package of diapers, mothers of Raquels are sent home with complimentary packages of eye shadow and lipstick.

Raven
A large, frightening, black bird that eats bugs.

Rebecca
Ancient Hebrew term referring to a heifer. Moo. Moo.

Regina
Means "queen." Handy when you want to be *sure* you'll raise a brat.

Renée
Means "reborn." This name is popular among believers of reincarnation. Many parents with December babies use this name as if Jesus were reborn on Christmas. On Easter Sunday, these goofs celebrate Jesus' third birth.

Don't Name Your Baby

Rhonda
Means "noisy."

Robin
Batman's adorably helpless protégé. Or a worm-eating animal with a brain the size of a pea.

Rori
Unique? Most people will just think, "Oh, Laurie, with an 'R'."

Rose
Very popular among children who smell.

Roxanne
A name that looks terrific on a waitress's nametag.

Ruby
To quote Shaggy's best friend, "Ruby, ruby roo!" Ruby seems to show up most often in television and film as a standard for any Southern Black woman over eighty.

Ruth
People will think she has a lisp.

Sabrina

Some eggheads might associate this name with the great Roman goddess, but for everyone else what will come to mind is television's teenage witch.

Sally

Charlie Brown's sadist sister; a favorite of steel town uniforms and bowling shirts.

Samantha

Your obnoxious brother-in-law will call her Sammy Sosa; most everyone else will just call her Sam. That racist down the street who thinks he's funny will call her "little Black sambo," and your grandmother will never understand why you choose to give your daughter a boy's name.

Sandra

Common popular reference: That hot chick from *Grease* who had everybody tricked into thinking she had a semblance of moral rectitude when in fact she was as easy as an automatic transmission.

Sarah

Biblical history: A woman whose most noteworthy accom-

Don't Name Your Baby

plishment seems to be that she was still kickin' it with Abraham when they were both past ninety.

Sasha
When she has braces and somebody asks her name, she'll just spit all over them.

Savannah
A stiflingly humid swamp with a couple of buildings, cross-dressers, and murderers.

Selena
Like calling your boy Elvis in the fifties. It seems like a touching tribute to Selena now, but don't you think adults named Elvis are tired of being asked about it? How's about you call her Sting?

Shana/Shayna/Sheena
Of the jungle?

Shania
That don't impress me much.

Girls' Names

Sharon
Ironically, most Sharons are stingy.

Sheila
Timeless schoolyard chant:
Sheila, Sheila! I want to feel ya'.

Shelby
A clumsy, awkward-sounding name that fits best on people who are shaped like eggs.

Shelly
Timeless schoolyard chant:
Smelly Shelly, kiss and telly.
Give her a nickel and she'll show you her belly.

Sherry
Timeless schoolyard chant:
Sherry, Sherry, dingleberry.
Uses Nair 'cause her chest is hairy.
Kids can be so cruel.

Shirley
A nametag worn by more proud diner hash slingers than

any other. Good 'ol Shirley. Don't you just want to give her a pat on the butt? *Likely nickname:* Squirrely.

Sierra
Most of the world thinks of this word in reference to mountains or fish, not little girls.

Simone
Oooh. Get that girl a beret. How desperately pompous of you.

Skye
As long as you're arrogantly misspelling nature, how about Grasse or Laque?

Skylar
Court magician of the Minivan Royalty, Skylar makes rain when Ashley's sandbox is dry, and shines an everlasting sun on Brittany's radiant brow (see page 50).

Sophia
A sophism is a lie and a sophist is a liar.

Girls' Names

Stacy

One of those unfortunate names that does not have an "adult" version. To move up the corporate ladder, most Stacys change their name to Hank. Those who choose to keep their name, end up stuck in low paying, dead-end jobs at Chuck E. Cheese and Toys-R-Us.

Stephanie

The sound dogs make when they sneeze.

Summer

An honorary member of the Daycare Sovereignty, Summer serves as the court magician, causing blossoms to bow to Courtney, and birds to sing for Lindsey (see page 50).

Susan

If you don't already know a Susan, maybe you're not alive. Once beautiful and lyrical, the name Susan has been so overused that it now smells worse than a moldy dishrag.

Suzanne

Snotty form of Susan. Girls named Suzanne spend all their time thinking they're "like, so much better than Susans." And they're, like, so not!

Don't Name Your Baby

Sydney
Historical origin: When a confused grandfather volunteered to fill out the birth certificate, he accidentally wrote his own name.

Tabitha
A good name for a cat.

Tamara
Tamara, and Tamara, and Tamara creeps in this petty pace from day to day . . . see you tommorra', Tamara! Are you ready for a lifetime of these bad jokes?

Tammy
There are some things from which a name can never recover, and five pounds of eyeliner is one of them.

Tanya
What's this? The feminine version of Tonya? Even as a double feminine, this name is still as girlish as a jockstrap.

Tara
This name's greatest attribute is that it is pretty easy to say. Unfortunately, it promotes a verbal laziness that lands

most Taras in the office of the school speech pathologist.

Tatiana

Titty-what???

Taylor/Tyler

Listen, every boy in the neighborhood is named Taylor or Tyler. Do we really need to name the girls Taylor and Tyler, too?

Teresa

Mother Teresa has shamed us all, and any girl who can find her way out from the shadow of this name is probably too good to be much fun or too bad to raise. *See* Names Your Child Will Never Live Up To.

Tia

Your daughter will always wonder if you meant to name her this, or if you just got distracted while filling out the birth certificate and never finished.

Tierra

Yeah, there's nothing sadly affected about naming your kid after a piece of costume jewelry.

Don't Name Your Baby

Tiffany

Famed leader of The Trailer Park Underground. Once among the elite of the Minivan Royalty, Tiffany was banished by Brittany, Ruler of The Desperately Pretentious Suburban Elite for being "two-faced" and "bossy" (see page 50).

Tina

Timeless schoolyard chant:

> *Tina, Tina. She'll _____ your weena.*
> *(insert verb here)*

Tonya

(weep, weep) My . . . skate . . . (sniffle, sniffle) . . . it's *untied* . . . (weep, weep).

Toni

Boy name! Boy name!

Tori

A name growing in popularity due to stick-figure rock star Tori Amos. Political Tories were rushed out of America in rowboats after the revolution. *Likely nickname:* Whorey.

Girls' Names

Tracy

A name that comes with its own set of pigtails and saddle shoes. Even into their forties, most Tracys show affection to boys by kicking them.

Trisha

What's the matter? You don't like her enough to give her a full name? *Likely nickname:* Trish the dish.

Tyra

I prefer Goodyear, but my mechanic suggests Michelin.

Ula/Uma/Una

OOGAH BOOGAH!

Valerie

A one- or three-syllable name. One of those oddities that do not fit properly into a chorus of "Happy Birthday."

Vanessa

Timeless schoolyard chant:
> *Vanessa, Vanessa, she'll let you undress 'er.*

Names Sure to Keep Your Girl Jobless
(a.k.a. So You Want To Raise a Porn Star?)

Believe it or not, a day will come when your little sweetheart will want to be taken seriously, and be sure she won't appreciate you creating her own personal glass ceiling. There's nothing more ridiculous and defeating than a judge named Bambi, a governor named Candy, or a CEO named Barbie. Don't recognize those combinations? That's because they don't exist.

Bambi
Barbie
Blossom
Candy
Cindy
Gigi
Josie
Joy
Lilly
Lulu

Peekaboo
Raquel
Star
Sugar
Tabatha
Tiffany
Xena, Princess
Warrior

Budding CEO

Girls' Names

Veronica

Everybody knows Veronica as the stuck-up vixen from *Archie Comics*. Why dangle it in front of those old Archie fans? They have enough sexual frustration as it is.

Victoria

Victoria is too pretentious, so she'll go by Vicki, a name with all the shape and rhythm of a work boot.

Virginia

Wishful thinking. *See* Names Your Child Will Never Live Up To.

Wendy

"Say, Wendy? Think we'll ever get to change out of these overalls and leave Out-of-Fashion Land?"

Winona

What are her friends going to call her for short? Win? Nona? Tree?

Zoe

Always last in line and back of the class.

Boys' Names

Aaron
Girl name! Girl name!

Abraham
Once a name evoking the power and dignity of our greatest president, one is now more likely to see "Abraham" sewn onto the chest of a school janitor's shirt or scribed into a bowling ball.

Adam
You're bound to instill in young Adam a sense of righteous priority as you tell him that he's named after "the first man." Prepare to pick up the pieces when a second-grader named Adam convinces yours that he was actually named after him.

Adolf
People will hate him before they even meet him.

Adrian
Yo, Adrian! Hope you like lame Stallone impressions. You're going to hear a lot of them.

Boys' Names

Alan

Not really a girl's name, but sounds close enough! Girl's name! Girl's name! It has been reported that as a child, Alan Greenspan was nicknamed "Alan the alien" by his friends in Econ 101. In retaliation he raises interest rates whenever he feels the bullies are making too much money. Curious fact: Twenty-five percent of all game show hosts are named Alan; the other 75 percent are named Wink.

Albert

Hey! Hey! Hey! It's Fat Albert!

Aldo

Great for babies born with a single eyebrow or hairy knuckles. Many babies born with pinky rings will request this name themselves.

Alexander

The world's most celebrated hegemonic egomaniac. Widely credited with uniting the world under his expansive armpits, Alexander probably wasn't well liked by those he conquered or those he ruled. Most modern day Alexanders claim to be captain of their football teams—they're not. *Likely nickname:* Alexander the geek.

Don't Name Your Baby

Alfred

See Names that Come with a Scent: mothballs.

Amos

Amos is a name meant for a 300-pound, neckless, overalled farm hand. Your baby would suffocate under a name that big.

André

So you're going to raise a hairdresser!

Andrew

Like it or not, everyone is going to call him Andy. As such, he'll adopt the nicknames Handy Andy, Candy Andy, or, if he's partial to puffy shirts and walks with a swagger, Dandy Andy.

Some famous Andrews you don't want to name your child after: Andrew Dice Clay (unfunny and offensive comedian), Andrew Lloyd Webber (unfunny and offensive composer), Andrew Cunanan (unfunny and offensive serial killer), Hurricane Andrew (unfunny and offensive hurricane).

Famous Monkey Names

Fictional monkeys have a fine tradition of original and intelligent namings. And don't fall victim to the prideful notion that somehow a monkey name is not noble or intellectual enough for your baby. Monkeys are very intelligent creatures. Some monkeys can do sign language. Can you do sign language? Some monkeys can ride a unicycle. Can you ride a unicycle? Consider evolving one of these excellent simian monikers into your family's banana tree. With an open mind, you're bound to have a monkey-good time naming and raising your own little Bubbles.

Abu	**Chim Chim**	**Magilla**
Beppo	**Curious**	**Mojo Jojo**
Bingo	**George**	**Rafiki**
Bobo	**Finsty**	**Zira**
Bonzo	**Grape Ape**	
Bubbles	**Koko**	

Not included in this list is Tarzan's friend named Cheetah because calling a monkey Cheetah is just plain stupid.

Source: http://www.citizenlunchbox.com/monkey/links.html

Don't Name Your Baby

Angel

Meow. *See* Names Your Baby Won't Live Up To.

Angelo

Meowo.

Anthony

Yo, Anthony! It's spaghetti day! Every joker Anthony meets will refer to him as "Antony" and follow that cleverness with their favorite scene from *Goodfellas* or *The Godfather*.

Ariel

For a boy? *Likely nickname:* The Little Mermaid.

Arthur

In a survey of 1000 computer programmers, none said they would name a child Arthur, claiming, "the name sounds nerdy. Even to me!" The programmers then snorted, pushed their glasses further up their noses, and got back to their comic books.

Ashton

You are likely to call him Ash. His friends are likely to call him Ass.

Boys' Names

Aubry

A handy name to choose if you thought you were going to have a girl and for expediency's sake, you already filled out the birth certificate with your chosen name of Audry. Simply scribble a "b" over the "d" and you've got yourself a boy name!

Austin

Crime rate per 100,000: murder 7.2, robbery 301, burglary 1377, car theft 768.

—Source: FBI Uniform Crime Reports 1994.

Avery

Some parents are under the impression that an unused name is thus an "exclusive" name. Sometimes, though, people don't use a name because it's lousy. *Likely nickname:* Gravy.

Barry

Likely nicknames: Barry the fairy, Dinglebarry, Bare-ass.

Beau

It's time to take a look in the mirror. Beau literally means "handsome" and everybody knows it. So you're gambling. It's like being bald and stuck with the nickname

Don't Name Your Baby

"Curly." You know what everyone's thinking when you're introduced. They're thinking, "Hey! That guy's named Curly, but he's got no hair!" And that kid's named Beau, but . . . why tempt fate? *See* Names Your Baby Will Never Live Up To.

Benjamin
Likely nickname (after the renowned Irish writer of homo-erotica)*:* Ben Dover.

Bill/Billy
Boys named Billy tend to look good in checked shirts, have bug collections, and like the taste of dirt.

Blaire
Timeless schoolyard chant:
> *Blaire, Blaire with greasy hair*
> *and tread marks on his underwear!*

Experts estimate 46,783 derivatives of this verse.

Blake
This kid is a smart-ass. Unless you want to field a lot of calls from pissed-off teachers, forget about this one. *Likely nickname:* Blake the fake.

Boys' Names

Bob

The name of the American proletariat. In some towns, all the men are named Bob. In certain academic circles it is believed that the Ancient Latin term for "everyman" was "Bob." One day we will see the end of all originality and spark of creativity, and on that day the faceless, genderless blob will rule. And that faceless, genderless blob shall be called Bob. *See* Bob Names (page 102).

Brad

Hardware, not a name. Brads avoid the popcorn line at movie theatres, preferring instead the taste of Twizzlers and Ju Ju Bees. Brads are not above accepting a bag of half-eaten popcorn from patrons leaving the theatre.

Brandon

Possibly Untrue Hollywood Story: During the seventies, television's ABC incubated thousands of Brandons for later use on their Friday night family sitcoms. Most of the Brandons turned out hideously ugly and instead ended up working in the commissary.

Brendon

A cheap knock-off of Brandon in the same spirit as those

Don't Name Your Baby

cereals sold in discount stores that have names like Jeerios or Brosted Blakes.

Brennan
Brandon to Brendon to Brennan—a final step in the degeneration of a name.

Brent/Brett
These names are essentially the same for those who'll be forced to use them. Brents and Bretts will often "trade places" for a week, cleverly fooling teachers and family members.

Brian
A name that despite its age and common usage has virtually no history. How is it possible that so popular and WASPish a name has never shown up in the White House or at the head of the Senate? Maybe your baby will be the first. Or maybe he'll be just another in a long line of underachieving Brians.

Brock
A name better suited to a fifty-year-old actor trying to stay in show business by playing tough guys on TNT. *See* Names That Come With a Scent: Grecian Formula.

Boys' Names

Brody

Likely nickname: Toady.

Bruce

True Hollywood Story: When television created a series based on the comic book *The Incredible Hulk*, they changed the name of the main character from Bruce to David because they felt Bruce sounded too effeminate for a superhero.

Bryce

Why don't you wise up? A kid named Bryce is not going to be content living in a ranch house and riding in a Hyundai. This kid will be more than happy to dump you for some loaded parents the first chance he gets.

Caleb

Sounds cool doesn't it? Erudite without being pompous, right? In Hebrew it means "dog."

Calvin

1. Since most of this book concerns predestination, I feel compelled to reveal that in Latin this name means "bald."
2. Eventually Calvin will have an identity crisis when he learns that hard work is almost never rewarded in America.

Don't Name Your Baby

Cameron/Cam
Likely nicknames: Cameroon, Spameron/Spam.

Carl
"Good dog, Carl."

Carter
One who drives a cart. Like a cab driver. You're aiming high now!

Casey
Chuga, chuga. Chuga, chuga. Chuga, chuga. Woo! Woo!

Chad
Likely nickname: Pregnant Chad.

Chance/Chase
Not only will your baby be a frat boy, but he'll wear turtlenecks and date only aspiring newscasters. When he makes his millions, and he will, he'll claim to have been adopted and cut off all association with you. Chances and Chases are jerks.

Charles
Prince Charles has ruined this name for everyone.

Names of Satan's Pawns

You don't have to be a Rosemary to give birth to the Antichrist these days. And you don't have to settle for traditional demon seed monikers, either. However, if you want to insure you've given your little devil the head start he'll need on the road to world domination, give him a name people will recognize as pure evil right from the start.

Adolph
Carrie
Damian
Freddy
Jason
Jezabel
Lucifer

Mao
Norman
Pol Pot
Regan

garlic

Don't Name Your Baby

Charlie

You know what your in-laws will be thinking when staring at that single hair protruding from your baby's big round head.

Chaz

Likely nickname: Spaz.

Christian

Okay, imagine this: a man from Tibet introduces you to his son, Buddhist. Wouldn't you find *that* a little odd?

Christopher

The first other Christopher your boy will encounter will be Christopher Robin, the effeminate, delusional, matriarchal priss of Winnie the Pooh fame.

Clarence

Means "lukewarm water." *Annoying phrase likely to haunt you both:* Hey! There's a pubic hair on my soda can!

Clay

A wet lump of Clay. Malleable. Moldable. Invertebrate. Spineless.

Biblical Names

Most parents claim to be after unique and original names, but too often they end of up with the same old thing. Oddly, many parents use as their primary resource, the best baby book of all, the *Holy Bible*. However, from the discriminating choices of some parents, one would think that the *Bible* contains only twenty or thirty names. In fact, the apostles and prophets had plenty of company and the *Bible* names them all. Numbers has page after page of fine names that baby books never seem to heed. So Gad and Zebulum sit unused while Jason and John are tossed around like confetti. Perhaps with the resource below, parents will begin to stretch their religious passions to include all that The Good Book has to offer.

Abihu	**Hepher**	**Puvah**
Ard	**Hoglah**	**Selophehad**
Balak	**Izri**	**Shimron**
Barzillai	**Kareah**	**Tola**
Bukkiah	**Nadab**	**Zadok**
Gad	**Obed**	**Zebul**
Gershon	**Og**	**Ziba**
Hakkoz	**Othni**	

Don't Name Your Baby

Clifford
Yup. Yup. Consistently scores in the bottom 10 percent on intelligence tests. A big, dumb, red name.

Clinton
Hey, I understand; I voted for him too. But this name's been soiled worse than a blue party dress.

Cody/Kody
Hee haw! Is your little suburbanite gonna grow up to be a cowboy? Isn't that cute . . . for a while? Just think of him at forty in a baby blue, tasseled rancher's outfit with furry chaps on his way to his job at the convenience store. Giddy-up!

Colby
Like the cheese. Mmm, orangy goodness.

Cole
A merry old soul! A big, fat, round name for a big, fat, round kid. Ho! Ho! Ho!

Colin
Of or relating to the human body's vilest organ.

Boys' Names

Connor

In Ireland, men caught in the act of bestiality were banished from their villages and branded Connor, meaning "one who loves wolves." Really. Look it up.

Corey

Girl name! Girl name! In the early nineties, the Screen Actors Guild advised all actors under eighteen to change their names to Corey. *Tiger Beat* actually changed its name to *Corey Beat* for two years. But like all fads, Corey went the way of the Bay City Rollers. Yonder.

Craig

Sounds like a crack in the cement or a rip in the seat of your pants. *Likely nickname:* Craig the faig.

Curtis

Curt is . . . Curt is what? *Likely nickname:* Dirtiss.

Dakota

How very arrogant and nouveau chic of you to name your child after an entire people your nation defeated.

Don't Name Your Baby

Dallas

Crime rate per 100,000: murder 27.8, robbery 666, burglary 1680, car theft 1664.

—Source: FBI Uniform Crime Reports 1994.

Damian

Satan worship is a private, family matter. There's no need to advertise it. Besides, he'll probably just torment you to insanity, anyway.

Daniel

An ancient name dating back to the biblical Daniel. Of course, famous and inspirational Daniels of the twentieth century include . . . well . . . okay, not a lot of impressive Dans out there. Who knows? Maybe your kid will break the trend.

Darrell

And my other brother . . .

Darren

What kind of controlling, misogynistic geek marries a witch and then doesn't let her practice witchcraft in the house? *Likely nickname:* Derwood.

Boys' Names

David

This is my name and I wrote this tasteless book. And if that isn't reason enough for you to stay away from this one, then you have a pitiable lack of self-respect. Hate mongering psychopaths who'll share your baby's name include David Berkowitz, David Koresh, David Duke.

Dax

Origin: Researchers have been able to track this name back to early 1963 when a woman coughed up a hairball while filling out her son's birth certificate.

> Destined for Dennis the Menace jokes all my growing days . . .

Dennis

Likely nickname: The Menace. Children named Dennis are seven times more likely to be diagnosed ADD—eight times if they have blond hair and buck teeth.

Denver

Crime rate per 100,000: murder 15.8, robbery 498, burglary 1518, car theft 1222. —*Source: FBI Uniform Crime Reports 1994.*

Don't Name Your Baby

Denzel

Great at clearing up pimples!

Devin

At first glance this name will always look like "Devil." Imagine looking under the Christmas tree and seeing all those nametags with "Devil" scrawled out in blood red ink. What are you going to name your next kid? Satal? Lucifred?

Dexter

Gee whiz. Better buy him a big pair of glasses and a propeller beanie! *See* Why Don't You Just Name Him "Kick My ass?" (page 124).

Dick

The name for which this book was written! Second grade gold! The f-word of baby names! Dick has a classic lampoon value that will never spoil with age. Beauty, clarity, simplicity: Dick. Dick the dick. Dickhead. Dickbrain. Dick is a dick. Dick. Dick. Dick. Nice fraternity pin Dick. Tricky Dick. Tricky Dick and his trick dick. Someone get me my secretary. I need her to take Dick-tation. Tell her to bring me my Dick-tionary. I want to look up Dick-tators. Hey!

Boys' Names

How about that prostate doctor, Dick Hertz! I think it's really VD. Call Dr. Dick Burns! Hey look out for that Dick Armey! Dick! Dick! Dick! What a dick!

Dirk

Likely nickname: Dirk the jerk.

Dominic

He'll go by Dom, which people will mishear as Tom. So you might as well call him Tom . . . but that's an ugly, boring name.

Donald

Best known as Mickey's pantless, jerky friend who spits when he talks and gets way too bent out of shape about everything.

Donovan

They'll call him Mellow Yellow. Quite right, slick.

Doug

Likely nickname: The bug.

Don't Name Your Baby

Drake
Likely nickname: The flake.

Drew
Not a name so much as the past tense of draw. *Likely nickname:* Pooh.

Dustin
You know what dust is? It's the flaked remains of human skin. So what are you naming him after? Human remains? The act of brushing away human remains?

Dylan
The rustic, earthy poetry of this name will surely fade a bit every time it is shouted across a soccer field or in the plastic playlands of suburbia.

Earl
Seventy-five percent of all Earls have mustaches. The other 25 percent have mouton chop sideburns. All Earls have at least one "Earl" belt buckle.

Edward
Babies named Edward tend to be born with a clear part.

Boys' Names

They are likely to wear ties to school and attempt to convince their friends to join the Young Republicans. They are also likely to get beat up a lot.

> "They called me Smelliot at school today."

Elijah
Likely nickname: Smellijah.

Elliot
Likely nickname: Smelliot.

Eric
Exclusively for redheaded gangly types who dress up like tarot card characters for Halloween.

Elliot

Ernest/Ernie
Naming a baby Ernest or Ernie has been known to trigger a gene that increases ear size. Hey, Bert!

Ethan
Evokes a time of revolution and noble rebellion. It also evokes an image of silly hats and ponytails. That brings to

Dog or Baby?

Get him a bone and register him at PetSmart. Many of these names have recently become quite popular, especially among city-dwellers—so have child leashes. Could there be a connection? Further, not only have more children been named as if they were dogs, more and more dogs are being named as if they were people. Could dogs be plotting our overthrow? Need the final piece of the puzzle? In the cities, where the revolution will inevitably begin, conspirator/slave humans have been seen carrying little plastic baggies that reportedly contain their "master's" poop. Fight the power, fellow humans. If you believe in the future of our species, avoid these canine names.

Coco	**Rex**
Lassie	**Rover**
Leo	**Scooby**
Max	**Simba**
Prince	**Toto**
Quincy	

mind the image, and, of course, the voice of Michael Bolton. Okay, that's enough. Pick a different name.

Eugene

Interesting fact: No Eugenes have ever carried a ball more than five yards in an organized football game. Most tend to be tackled by their own linemen.

Felix

Felix, el gato! El ludico, ludico gato! Your baby's likely to be a fastidious little twerp.

Forrest

Not so much a name as place with lots of trees and bugs.

Frank

Most Franks develop a taste for *Matlock* and fried liver before they even reach puberty. Let me be Frank. Why? Who would want to? A rank name with a stank and you can put that in the bank.

Fred

"Hi. Will you go on a date with me? My name's Fred." Sounds a lot like, "Hi. Will you go on a date with me? I'm

Don't Name Your Baby

goofy looking and dopey." A name that's sure to keep your baby stag for life.

Garrett

Timeless schoolyard chant:

Garrett the ferret,
he smells just like a carrot!

Gary

Timeless schoolyard chant:

Gary the fairy,
his palms are raw and hairy!

George

Duh, George . . . do I get to tend the rabbits? Do I? Sure. You and I know George was the smart one, but hardly anyone else can keep that straight.

Gerald

A very weird kid. Boys named Gerald are twice as likely to develop an embarrassing twitch and store their parents in a refrigerator after their mysterious disappearance.

Boys' Names

Giovanni

Swarthy and sweaty. This name just oozes hair products. It sounds like the roar of a sports car and reeks of Brut.

Gordon

In Spanish this name means "fatso."

Graham

Likely nickname: The Cracker. Not a funny nickname if you happen to be a Southern racist.

Grant

Timeless schoolyard chant:
  Grant, Grant, underpants!

Greg

If it weren't a name it would refer to skin tags. "Eeew. I've got more gregs growing on my butt again, honey. Can you get the lighter and burn off these gregs?"

Harley

You're going to name your son after a motorcycle ridden primarily by filthy, overweight losers?

Don't Name Your Baby

Harold

Most Harolds tend to marry women named Gladys. So until Gladys picks up, you might want to shy away from this one.

Harrison

It sounds so sharp and handsome, but face it: people are going to call him Harry whether you like it or not. Good old Harry. Your son.

Hayden

Sounds enough like "hating" to be confused as a joke-name implying a dislike for your surname. Your hard-of-hearing relatives are going to think you have a sick sense of humor.

Henry

An odd dental condition that usually arrives during his fifth year as Henrys tend to contract Heehawitus. Symptoms include hayseed growths protruding from between the teeth and a love of country music.

Howard

Likely nickname: Dirty Howie.

Hunter

Meaning: One who affirms his masculinity by sitting around waiting for small animals to come by so he can shoot them.

Ian

A name that first appeared in the eighteenth century as a blatant misspelling of John.

Isaac

A ridiculously spelled name that most people associate with the bartender on *The Love Boat* rather than the biblical character.

Ivan

Guarantees back hair and a love of professional wrestling. Most Ivans tend to be overweight from eating their house pets.

Jack

Hungry! Hungry Jack! Famous Jacks include the addle-brained Jack who trades a cow for a handful of beans. Later he climbs

Don't Name Your Baby

a beanstalk, rips off a giant and kills him. What a jerk. *Likely nickname:* Jack off. Black Jack (unless he actually is Black).

Jackson
Unless the father's name is Jack, this name will make no sense to anybody. If the father's name is Jack, what is he? Some kind of ego-maniac? Muhammad is the most popular name in the world and I have yet to meet a Muhammadson. Get over yourself, Jack!

Jacob
Proud biblical legacy: Screwed his brother out of his birthright and was tricked into marrying the homely sister of his fiancée.

Jake
Slick guys, those Jakes. A Jake is as likely to write you a bad check as he is to sell you cheap siding. If you name your kid Jake, send him my way. He probably owes me money. *Likely nickname:* Jake the snake.

Jalen
A Star Trek name if there ever was one. Your kid will be appreciated at Trekie conventions all over the country.

Bob Names

Bob is the name of the American proletariat, the default name for all boys and men who choose not to convey too much personality— just faces in the crowd. Bob and other such names ensure a stable lifestyle, tidy hairstyles and regular bowels. Bob names exude the spice of Corn Flakes and the excitement of the Midwest. They roll on like a tractor down an expressway, dignified and measured, waving proudly to the passing cars, "You go on with your speed, fellas. I'm a Bob guy and I'll get there. Slow and steady but sure enough, I'll get there." Try to stay awake as you read following list of Bob names.

Bill	**Dennis**	**Ron**
Bob	**Ed**	**Ted**
Brad	**George**	**Todd**
Brian	**Jim**	**Tom**
Charlie	**Joe**	
Chris	**Phil**	

Don't Name Your Baby

Everywhere else he'll just be the kid whose parents must be freaks.

James

They will call him Jimmy. They will. And he'll like it.

Jason

So overused in the early nineties that the government now requires a special permit to use this name. You know how a dollar bill looks when it has been in circulation too long? That's how this name appears to the rest of the world.

Jay

A letter, not a name.

Jeffrey

Boys named Jeffrey tend to pick their noses and be overly concerned with the part in their hair. Most Jeffreys grow up to be accountants, but a lucky few remain unemployed.
United States Presidents named Jeffrey: 0
Phony giraffes named Jeffrey: 1

Boys' Names

Jeremy
Likely nickname: Germy.

Jerome
How original. Just see Gerald, it's the same damn name anyway.

Jesse
A name inextricably linked to America's most famous killer. Good choice.

Jim/Jimmy
As bland as a pair of chinos and a brown belt. As boring and predictable as a train ride through Nebraska. Big Jim. Jimmy-boy. Nothing too exciting here.

Joe
Your baby will think you didn't have time to come up with a good name, so you went with the first one that came to mind. Joes don't always underachieve, but they are well aware that their parents expect them to. Babies named Joe tend to be fat and bald . . . forever.

Don't Name Your Baby

John
    A excellent way to ensure the obscurity of your child's very existence would be to give him a name that just about everybody else has.

Jordan
    Good idea. Not nearly enough people named their boys Jordan during the Bulls' run of the nineties. We sure could use a few more.

Joshua
    If it weren't a name, it would refer to a wet, moldy rag. Squish, squash.

Julian
    Girl name! Girl name!

Justin
    Likely nicknames: If he's always late, they'll call him Justin-time. If he's a lawyer, they'll call him Justin-case. Why don't *you* just call him something else?

Keaton
    There was a time when great men and women would be

Boys' Names

honored by seeing their surnames turned into first names. Now we have the surnames of fictional characters from sitcoms being honored this way. You don't want to assist in this cultural degradation, do you?

Keith

Means "forest," but most people associate this name with David Cassidy's role on *The Partridge Family*.

Kelly

Girl name! Girl name!

Kelvin

The name clearly originated on a misspelled birth certificate. Your Kelvin will have to spend far too much of his life correcting people and he'll eventually just change his name to Calvin or Kevin anyway.

Ken/Kenny

Barbie's boring, well-groomed eunuch "friend." A lot of party talk centers around Ken's sexual orientation, but in his anatomical state such speculation is entirely irrelevant.

The Dot Com Revolution

Fashion in naming children is often a product of economics and politics. The practice of naming one's children after the privileged class has been going on for centuries. Victoria and Elizabeth were, of course, most popular during the reigns of the English queens. The peons, if they can't make a decent living, ought to at least be able to pretend their children are dignified. Now that our economic heroes are the young pioneers of cyberspace, names that once used to guarantee lonely Saturday nights, names fathers used to slap on their runts to toughen them up, have now become stylish and coveted. Soon pocket protectors will start showing up at French fashion shows. Name your boy one of these and be sure to pick up some masking tape for his glasses.

Arthur	**Fred**
Bill	**Graham**
Bob	**Jerome**
Brad	**Martin**
Craig	**Randall**
Dirk	**Spencer**
Dexter	

Boys' Names

Kerry

Did you know that the Ring of Kerry surrounds the Dingle Peninsula? Not exactly, but it sounds so funny!

Kevin

Irish Americans who name their sons Kevin have an inflated sense of cultural self and little imagination or originality.

Kirk

Likely nickname: Kirk the jerk.

Kurt

More of an expletive than a name. As the name implies, most parents who chose Kurt didn't have enough time for a longer, better name.

Kyle

If it weren't a name it would refer to the act of coughing up phlegm.

Lance

Timeless schoolyard chant:
> *Lance, Lance, watch him dance,*
> *'cause he got dirty underpants!*

Don't Name Your Baby

Lawrence
Forget the pretense. Your in-laws will be calling him Larry from the start. From there he's only a monogrammed button-down away from a janitorial job.

Leonardo
Do you really want to name your baby after a perpetually pubescent movie star you have a crush on? Isn't that going to be emotionally confusing for you both during his Oedipal phase?

Leslie
Girl name! Girl name!

Lloyd
A ridiculously spelled name. An unusually high percentage of Lloyds grow superfluous third nipples.

Logan
Probably won't live past thirty.

Louis
How many corrupt, vulgar kings need sully this name for you to let it be? *Likely nickname:* Sweet Lou!

Boys' Names

Lucas

Timeless schoolyard chant:
Lucas pucus, smells like mucus.

Luke

Likely nickname: Puke.

Mark

1) A blemish. A scratch. A scar. When you see a mark on your skin, you get the darn thing removed! 2) Although the New Testament clears this one up a bit, Mark is actually derived of Mars, the nasty god of war.

Marshall

A very bossy kid. Often thinks he's running things when other kids are trying their best to ignore him.

Martin

Martin Luther King did everything he could to save this name. Some historians claim that much of his civil rights campaign was actually a symbolic crusade to save Martin from its nerdish tradition. While his work was noble, it remains unfinished: Martin is still only a name as cool as the computer geek who bears it.

Don't Name Your Baby

Mason

Yeah, this job doesn't hold the prestige it once did.

Mathew/Matt

As in doormat. A metaphor that all mean girls know and use to their advantage.

Maurice

Likely nicknames: Some people call him the Space Cowboy; some call him The Gangster of Love.

Max

Bow wow! Sit boy! Sit! Heel! Boys named Max tend to relieve themselves on the morning paper and are distracted by passing cars.

Melvin

C'mon! You don't really want to name him Melvin! Your late Uncle Melvin will understand. He didn't like the name either.

Boys' Names

Micah

Here's another table for micah. Or is that a Formica table? Ah! Ha! Ha! Ha!

Michael

An advantage in giving your child the most popular name in America is that he'll never feel too special.

Mitch

Likely nicknames: Mitch the bitch. Nervous boys tend to be called Mitch the twitch.

Morgan

Aye! She's a fine pirate name and a right-good whiskey. That it be, matey. That it be. Arrgh.

Nathan

Two famous sociopaths who'll share your baby's name: Nathan Detroit (fictional mobster), Nathan Leopold (non-fictional murderer).

Neil

An act akin to bowing, expressing one's subordination before another. Isn't your baby worthy?

Ole-time Baseball Players

Gone are those idyllic days of summer when a man named Hippo could prance proudly 'round the bags of the noble diamond. Gone are the days when players had names that smacked of heroism and dignity—names like Spud and Cool Papa, names that evoked a kind of grace and power that we hope to one day see in the strides of our children. Oh, that it were so simple. If only a name could a decent and splendid person make. Who can say? But to give your child so fine a designation as these would be a hint of what a man can be in the prime of his days.

Arky	Dizzy	Mookie
Baby Doll	Daffy	Pants
Boileryard	Enos	Pee Wee
Boo	Frenchy	Pie
Bugs	Gee	Pinky
Cletis	Happy	Smead
Cool Papa	Heinie	Snooks
Creepy	Honus	Spud
Cuckoo	Hoot	Suitcase

Boys' Names

Nicholas

Nicholas? Don't be Ridickolous! They'll call him Pickle-less. Or worse!

Noah

Do you think Noah was laughing on the Ark? When the heathens pulled their rowboats up to the Ark, do you suppose Noah told them to get lost? Seems Noah, besides being God's favorite at the time, might have been a bit of a jerk.

Nolan

A handy name for Texans since the registrar of birth certificates has had a "Nolan stamp" made for easier processing of the million Nolans he sees every day.

Norman

Not all Normans are hypochondriacs, some are just afraid they are.

Oliver

Insurance rates run higher for Olivers since they are more likely to get beat up.

Don't Name Your Baby

Owen

OWEN! (see *Throw Momma From the Train*)

Parker

One who parks. Like a valet. Doesn't sound so pretentious *now*, does it?

Patrick

If you're Irish, there's no way I'll be able to talk you out of this one. So go ahead. You were going to use it anyway.

Paul

In Latin, Paul means "small." The enduring connotation is obvious. When your Paul hits puberty he's bound to change his name to Jumbo or Gargantua.

Perry

Likely nickname: Perry the fairy.

Peter

Once referred to strength and determination or "rock;" now refers to the male member.
Timeless schoolyard chant:
> *Peter, Peter, booger eater!*

Boys' Names

Phillip

In ancient Greece, men caught in the act of bestiality were banished from their villages and branded "Phillip," meaning "one who loves horses." Really. Look it up.

Pierre

Maybe he'll wear a cute little beret while he performs manicures.

> Pierre, be a good boy and finish your cereal.

> Mom looks fabulous in red.

Preston

Means "priest's town." An entire town of priests. A whole town and nobody else around for miles. Hmmm.

Quincy

Meow. Comes with a pretty collar and a ball of yarn.

Quinn

Likely nickname: Dr. Quinn, Medicine Baby.

Names Your Baby Will Never Live Up To

Life is hard. So do you really want to set the bar so high right off the bat? Why not wait to see how your kid turns out. If he starts showing signs of super intelligence at five, there's still plenty of time to change his name to Albert (Einstein). Is he particularly peaceful? Surely little Jesus won't object to a couple of nameless years to ensure you've gotten it right. Either way you avoid the unsettling prospect of a three-hundred-pound Ghandi in camouflage playing gory video games.

Abraham	**Edison**	**Mary**
Adonis	**Elijah**	**Mohammad**
Angel	**Grace**	**Noah**
Buddha	**Ivory**	**Theresa**
Caesar	**Jesus**	**Venus**
Chastity	**Joy**	**Virginia**
Diana	**Luther**	

Boys' Names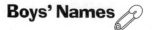

Ralph
Though all the characters on *Happy Days* seem dorky now, only Ralph was designed to be. *Likely nickname:* Puke.

Randall/Randy
If you call him Randall, kids will beat him up. If you call him Randy, teachers will think he has ADD.
"Hi, teacher! I'm Randy."
"Well try to control yourself."

Ray
A drop of golden sun. *Likely nickname:* Sweet Baby Ray (he won't make it to the White House with a nickname like that). Fay Ray.

Reginald
Archie Comics tried its best to salvage this one from the nerd pile. Toss it back.

Richard/Rick
Just look at Dick. You're not fooling anyone; the same problems apply.

Don't Name Your Baby

Robert

Nothing but Bob in a polyester suit.

Rodney

Oh. He won't get no respect. No respect.

Roger

A name for aging soap opera stars. Men named Roger tend to wear turtlenecks and be overly concerned with the whiteness of their teeth.

Ronald

You think you'll be naming him after our most popular, though most confused president, when in fact more people will associate your boy with a fast food–hawking clown.

Ross

Boys named Ross usually feel so bad that boys named Russ are so often called Ross that they change their name to Bobo.

Roy

Means "king." A throwback to a time when uneducated

peons could be fooled into subservience by any vulgarian clever enough to call himself "king."

Ruben

A sandwich, not a name.

Rudy

Timeless schoolyard chant:
> *Fruity Rudy, got a big booty.*

Russell

Since Russell sounds nerdy, he'll likely call himself Russ which people will mishear as Ross or Rust. Russ is likely to be quite a frustrated individual.

Ryan

Means "little king." Originally conceived as a reference to Roy's member. Timeless schoolyard chant:
> *Ryan, Ryan, can't stop cryin'.*
> *Peed in his pants and his dog is dyin'.*

Sam/Samuel

Despite all your protestations, they're going to call him Sammy. So if you can't

Don't Name Your Baby

handle that, don't name him Sam. *Likely nickname:* Sam I am.

Scott
Timeless schoolyard chant:
> *Snotty Scotty, pees a lotty.*
> *Wears a diaper 'cause he can't use the potty.*

Sean
Yet another blatant misspelling of John. Doesn't anybody in Ireland own a dictionary?

Sebastian
Means "comes from Sebastia." Very creative. Of course in your case, it's probably completely inaccurate. Maybe you should call him Springfieldite or Rochesterian.

Seth
People will think he has a lisp.

Shane
It'll be as if you'd taken a picture of him dressed as a cowboy for Halloween and permanently affixed it to his forehead.

Boys' Names

Shannon
Girl name! Girl name!

Sheldon/Sidney/Stanley
Most retirement homes have had a hard time keeping thirty-year-olds with these names from checking in early.

Ugh! Cursed with a 1970s girl name!

Shannon

Simon
I don't even know you, and already I want to beat up your kid.

Skylar
Sounds so hippy-cool and nonconformist, doesn't it? It means "scholar."

Spence/Spencer
Likely nickname: Dense/Denser.

Steven
A name with a fine tradition of men who have achieved fame and fortune despite their obvious lack of talent:

Don't Name Your Baby

Stephen King, Steve Jobs, Steve McQueen, Stevie Nicks.

Stuart
The name of a beloved suit-wearing mouse . . . or your child.

Tanner
One who tans hides. In the seventeenth century when leather workers couldn't think of any more names for their children, they'd just slap this one on a kid.

Taylor
It's strange how this name has risen in popularity and style. At what point did tailoring carry with it any degree of status? Even Tevya, the impoverished peasant from *Fiddler on the Roof*, didn't want his daughter to marry one.

Terrance/Terry
Timeless schoolyard chant:
> *Terry the fairy,*
> *his boyfriend broke his cherry!*

Theodore/Ted
Paranoid maniacs who'll share your baby's name: Ted Kaczynski, Ted Bundy, Ted Turner.

Why Don't You Just Name Him "Kick My Ass?"

Kids are cruel. Everybody says it, but to an expectant parent idyllic worlds of frolicking wide-eyed tots are all that await their little muffin. Face it. Kids will do or say anything to break your boy's spirit. Why give them more ammunition? Why hang a KICK ME sign on your own kid? Name your boy Adrian and watch him relive a nightmare every September as his name is called for attendance the first day of school: *"Adrian?" "Present." "Adrian, could you please stand up so that any new bullies will be sure to know who they should beat up?"* Some kids may actually come out of this stronger, but consider this: being named Sue may have made Johnny Cash tough, but it also put him behind the bars at San Quentin.

Adrian	Francis	Oliver
Arnold	Fred	Oscar
Barney	Garth	Ralph
Chaz	Gaylord	Seymour
Chase	Giles	Sheldon
Ernest	Irving	Simon
Eugene	Melvin	Waldo
Felix		

S
I
S
S
Y

Don't Name Your Baby

Thomas

As with Kevin and Patrick, if you're Irish you're probably going to name one of them Thomas anyway, so go ahead. Why'd you even buy this book?

Timothy

Most Timmy's never grow large enough to get on the big-kid rides at Disneyworld.

Todd

When women marry guys named Todd, they know they're settling. If Todd were not a name, it would refer to some sort of clothing fastener, like a button or snap.

Tony

Timeless schoolyard chant:
>Tony, Tony macaroni.
>Can't get a girl 'cause he looks too boney.

Travis

Hee-haw! Despite the name's relative lack of popularity, there is a Travis working in the stables of every racetrack in the United States.

Boys' Names

Trevor

Seemingly dashing, but ridiculous when scrawled on a Wal-Mart nametag.

Trey

Be prepared for your most clueless in-laws' remarks: "Trey? What kind of tray are we talking about here? Some sort of lunch tray? That's the baby's name?"

Troy

Most Troys end up playing characters named Clint when they eventually get contracted to a soap opera. So for most people, your boy might as well be named Clint.

Tucker

Likely nickname: (Uhh, do you even need to be told?)

Tyler

1) A historically accepted misspelling of Taylor, as if the office of births just got tired of correcting people. Most boys named Tyler lose points for spelling on the ACT before they even get to the questions. 2) One who lays tiles. Like a contractor. Sounds like you got yourself some really big dreams for your little guy, there.

Don't Name Your Baby

Victor
Timeless schoolyard chant:
Vic the dick, he makes the teacher sick.

Vince
Like sticking a permanent *Kiss Me. I'm Italian!* bumper sticker to his face.

Walter
What if he wants to be called Wally? Can you change his name then? Eh, what's the difference.

Warren
A name inextricably tied to the Court known primarily for its liberal take on social policy. Your father will hate him. *Likely nickname:* Borrin'.

Wayne
In Arkansas there is an organization called Guys Named Wayne United for the Return of Knit Ties to Stylishness and the Shelves of Sears.

William
William has a doll! William has a doll! Despite your preten-

Boys' Names

tious protestations, everyone's going to call him Billy, a freckly, lizard-catching kind of name.

Xavier

Bound to cause some damage to his self-esteem since he'll be unable to pronounce his name until he's twelve.

Zach

A Z name. Always last in line; always back of the class.

Zane

A Z name. Always last in line; always back of the class . . . but wearing a cute little cowboy hat.